CROCHET FOR

BEGINNERS

How to Master the Art of Crochet
and Learn Patterns with a Guide
Full of Illustrations, Pictures and
Processes for your Creations.

Table of Contents

Introduction

Have you ever wondered about the meaning of the word 'crochet' while holding your hook and crocheting? You fall in deep thinking and wonder about it. Well, I always did, and that's the reason I wanted to break it down for you "crochet lovers" to satisfy your curiosity and clear all confusion. The word crochet comes from the French word 'croche' which means 'to hook.' In the early 16th century, mastering this craft is an impression of being a well-bred and high-class woman. Crocheting was limited to the rich ladies, while those struggling to cope financially had to compete with knitting.

We do not know many things regarding the early origins of crochet because the ancient textiles that survived are very few. Some claim that originally, women used fingers to create loops and chains. Only later did they begin to use a tool very similar to the current hook, which was initially made of wood, bone, or bamboo and then in ivory and amber.

The oldest find, considered a precursor of crochet, comes from Jutland. It is a woolen cap that dates back to about 3100 years ago. However, primitive textile samples were found in every corner of the globe — the Far East, Asia, North and South America, and Europe.

Some scholars believe that Tambour work was at the origin of modern crochet. This technique was used in China. It required the use of a fine hook to weave threads through a netted background. Crocheting ended up being so popular in the 18th century. The skill is passed on from one generation to the next within families. The patterns then were simply taken into a picture and one needs to work and determine how to go around with the details.

However, at the beginning of the twenty-first-century, there has been a restoration of interest in hand-made and do-it-yourself, as well as excellent strides in the enhancement of the grades and the diversity of yarn. The art of crochet is one of the easiest skills that can be self-taught to learn the best ways to crochet and it is suitable for beginner or intermediate level.   The crochet technique is one of the oldest of the yarn processing techniques, considered very versatile and effective. Going back to the origins is not easy, as there are very few works found from distant eras.

The most current trends in the crochet sector are characterized by the creation of creative works without a basic design. In this way, crochet work is well on the way to becoming a fully-fledged art form.

Crochet became most notable when French nuns started to crate elaborate and delicate patterns. They were known to create complex lacework using very fine materials. They made table clothes used to cover the altar and adorn the church. It was said that the art of crochet was a closely guarded craft among the nuns. It became an integral part of life in the convent.

Over the next years, crochet found its way to Scotland and England. From the nuns, knowledge and skill were passed on to the upper class. Crochet circles were established among the ladies of the upper class. The work was no longer focused on delicate and complex lace but was just as elegant. During those times, the skill was limited among the upper class. The poor were not given the privilege to learn the craft.

During the Renaissance, both the upper and lower classes were practicing crochet. During this time, the ladies were using macramé, which is several fine threads knotted together. They made delicate lacework which became popular across Europe.

In the 1820s, crochet was introduced in Ireland. They used fine threads and made delicate work that imitated English lace. It became known as Irish lace. Over the next years, Irish lace became very popular in Europe, especially in the Balkans.

By the early 1900s, yarns changed from fine threadlike materials to something much thicker. Hook sizes also changed in order to accommodate the thicker yarns. Patterns started even more simplified, a deviation from the complex lacework in previous years. Crochet items progressed from laceworks such as table covers and church adornments, into something more practical such as gloves and scarves.

Modern Crochet

Today, crochet skills are too simple compared to how the French nuns used to make them. The craft has become widespread, but the skill levels can be compared to the level of primary school crochet. It is still considered fabulous but way below the level that crochet used to be.

Also, compared to decades ago, there are considerably fewer people who are interested in the craft. Learning the skill is no longer confined to closed groups, but fewer people are willing to try. Mass production and cheaper goods have made people less inclined to making their own socks or blankets.

However, there are still a considerable number of people who keep the skill ever-evolving. There are still people who wish to learn the craft.

Today's patterns are simpler. Popular ones include baby items such as sweaters, socks, bonnets, booties and blankets. Other items include afghans and adult wear such as scarves, socks and sweaters.

How to Read and Understand Crochet

Before learning to read crochet patterns, here are some important guidelines you need to remember.

Determine the crochet pattern you want to work with, and different patterns tell you which one will make a good scarf or a blanket. As a beginner, it is better to start with simple patterns first. The difficulty of the patterns is usually written under the title.

Establish the size of the finished product. It is better to take note of what size the product should be, especially in garments where measurements of different parts vary.

Are the materials complete? Buy the materials needed on the pattern you're going to work with. The type of yarn and the size of the crochet hook will be indicated on the pattern you chose.

Make sample swatches to identify the size of your project.

Know the stitches that will be used in making this pattern. They are most likely indicated at the beginning of the pattern, for example, includes; a single crochet, chain, half double crochet, slip stitch and many more.

Familiarize yourself with the keys and the abbreviations of techniques.

When you encounter an asterisk, the pattern is telling you that the step must be repeated.

Always begin with tying a slip knot onto your hook. Create a loop on the tip of the yarn, then slide it onto the crochet hook. Enfold the yarn back over the hook, then again pull it through the loop, and lastly pull the hook with one hand so both ends of the yarn are being held to tie a slip knot.

Start working step by step. The pattern will tell you how many chains you need to make. Steps are listed in order by the number of rows. Patterns always begin with a foundation chain that can be long or short.

Observe the numbers of stitches at the end of the row; the number informs you of how many stitches you'll be working with. Try to count your stitches every ten rows so you won't lose track of the pattern. You may also use a row counter, which can be an app or just manually write down the current row you're working with on a piece of paper. There is also a row counter that can be attached to the hook so you can click every time you finish a row.

Check if the pattern you are working on needs to be stitched together or blocked for the finishing step. Accessories like buttons and ribbons can also be added to the finishing touch.

When working with a crochet project, you need to follow a knitting pattern. And reading Crochet Patterns is like a code that must be deciphered. It may be an abbreviation or a term list, and as a beginner you might get intimidated when you cross path with these alien terms, but worry not! Just invest a little effort and soon enough all these foreign abbreviations for you will be a piece of cake.

Once you've chosen the pattern you want to do a hands-on, read all the information and take note of all the important details such as the abbreviations used, the type of stitches, yarn and materials that are needed, gauge information and sizing and other pattern note that needs to be jotted down.

Crochet terminology can be confusing for beginners when it comes to the dissimilarity between the US and UK abbreviations. Choose a pattern that is written in your language preference so you can get the right abbreviations.

Also, consider that pattern keys can be somewhat written in different ways; such as a term 3ch which means to make three chains can also be written as ch3. When you get to be comfortable with the abbreviations it will be easier for you to follow it given the slight changes.

Reading a crochet pattern is like learning a foreign language. It's quite tricky and when given the abbreviations of crochet terms below you may now start a basic pattern.

Make sure you pay attention to the terms used before purchasing patterns.

Reading crochet patterns can be fairly time-consuming at first, but you'll get used to it. Patterns are written in rows for items that are straight and flat, such as a square cloth. For something like a coaster, the pattern is written in rounds, this is the terminology we use.

Here is a row to practice reading - Row 1: Chain 12, dc in 2nd chain from the hook and across in each. Chain 1, turn (9)

Firstly, you can see that this is part of a pattern from a straight, flat item because the pattern refers to row 1. Next, chain 12 indicates that this is a chain made up of 12 chain stitches.

After this, there will be the half double crochet in chain number two from the hook (excluding the one carried by the hook). This is followed by the half double crochet in each stitch till the end of the row. Then you'll make one chain stitch for the following row.

Ready to try another one? This time we'll look at using asterisks. Here we'll focus on what part of the pattern needs to be repeated. Leave a piece of long thread, chain 21. Sc in the second chain and each across. (20 sts) - approximately 5" wide

Row 1: *single crochet in first st, double crochet in the next* repeat till the end. Chain 1 and turn (20 stitches)

Leave a long piece of yarn, then start your chain which will be 21 stitches long. Next make a single crochet in the second Ch stitch from the hook is (exclude the stitch with is attached to the hook) and also single crochet in each chain until the end of the row. It should be approximately 10 inches wide.

In row one, read the pattern carefully. You'll notice that there are only two asterisks. Everything in between the asterisks needs to get repeated till where the row ends. Firstly, the single crochet is done in the first stitch, then the double crochet is what follows in the next. Then, a single crochet in the first stitch comes again and is then followed by the double crochet. Follow through till the row ends. Make 1 chain stitch so that you can begin a new row.

This is just one example; you will learn as you go along. In addition to reading written patterns, you will also be able to use symbols to read patterns. Below is an elaborate list of common crochet symbols that are commonly used.

Key - UK

○ Chain

• Slip Stitch

✕ Double Crochet

┬ Half Treble Crochet

┬ Treble Crochet

┬ Double Treble Crochet

┬ Tripple Treble Crochet

Treble Crochet Cluster

Magic Loop

Key - USA

○ Chain

• Slip Stitch

✕ Single Crochet

┬ Half Double Crochet

┬ Double Crochet

┬ Treble Crochet

┬ Double Treble Crochet

Double Crochet Cluster

Magic Loop

Tools and Materials Needed for Crochet

Yarns

When you are beginning your crocheting journey, the first thing you will need, before doing anything, is to get all the supplies for your new hobby. There are a variety of different types of yarns and threads available for working in crochet. The wide variety includes options from alpaca yarn to banana silk and other alternative fibers. Some fibers are easier to work with, and some provide a nice texture to the project. It all depends on the handling which you will get from practice. The most common fibers used for beginners are wool, cotton, and acrylic. All of these have a lot of advantages and disadvantages as well.

Wool: This type of yarn is easy to reuse and unravel. Because of this property, if you make a mistake, it can easily be reversed. It's easier to work with, but working in the summer with this yarn becomes uncomfortable. In the summer, you might want to try out other lighter options.

Cotton: This type of yarn is also easy to use, but it doesn't easily unravel. If you are a beginner, working with cotton may seem a little harder than wool. It is less elastic than others. On the other hand, if your project requires that it maintains its shape, then cotton is better. It is lighter than wood so you can work with this in the summer.

Acrylic: When you are a beginner, you are making a lot of mistakes, and your projects are not coming out as you want them too. You're wasting a lot of yarn, which can be expensive if you are using other types. Acrylic is cheap, and it comes in a variety of colors. Its main disadvantage is that it's quite weak. There's a chance of breakage in acrylic, so you have to be careful when crocheting your project. If you are working with acrylic and your project breaking apart, then you should switch to other yarns that won't give you such misery.

Crochet Thread

All these types mentioned above are types of yarns but also use crochet threads as well. They are much finer and thinner. Because of this, it is harder to work with. If you're more interested in doing light-weighted projects like lacy and open clothes, than starting from thread might be the option for you. Thread types come in cotton and acrylic.

People think it's difficult to work with thread, but that is not true. Here are some tips that can help you work with threads:

- As a beginner, user thicker size thread. Instead of using 30 to 20, use 3. Upgrade to those two sizes when you have developed your skills.
- Use a suitable hook according to your yarn size. A smaller number indicates a bigger hook, so doesn't get frustrated. The best one is the steel crochet hook.
- People confuse embroidery thread with crochet thread and buy that instead. Make sure you're buying a crochet thread.
- Draw your loops closer to the crochet head when working with crochet threads.
- To get good tension in your thread, hold the ends of the thread in your left hand.

Identifying yarn will become second nature to you once you get enough practice. After a while, you will be able to judge the type of yarn just by touching it. As a beginner, you will get all the information about the yarn on the yarn ball when you purchase it. It will have all the information that you need.

Additional tips

Yarn weight: One of the most important things to consider is the yarn weight. The sizes start from 1-7, with 1 being the thinnest and 7 being the thickest. If you are a beginner, then working with worsted weight yarn, which is number 3 yarn, is the best. It is of average thickness and provides you with enough grip.

Yarn color: when you are doing a big project, then, if you're using the same color, you have to buy a lot of yarn in that color. Don't make this decision by your eyes. Read the label on top of the yarn balls and match the color code between them. This will ensure that you have the same color.

Yarn texture: Avoid using extremely fancy yarns and stick to smooth yarns. Once you have developed the skill, you can move onto them.

Yarn price: Different fibers are available at different costs. It is smart to work with an inexpensive at first when you make a lot of mistakes. When comparing prices, people look out for yardage as well.

Crochet Hooks

To understand what hook will best suit you, you need to understand the parts of the hook first. It has three parts:

Head and throat: The hook at the end of the utensil is the head. Immediately beneath it, a shallow depression is formed, and because of it, it is called a throat. The throat guides the yarn inside the head. There are two types of head: tapered and inline. Tapered hook has a more rounded head, which does not seem in line with the rest of the body. Inline hook has a more pointed head, which does seem in line with the rest of the body. Whichever you choose, will depend on you. How to use both to understand which one suits you.

Shank

This is the part which denotes the size of the hook. The larger it is, the longer will the stitches you are making with it be. It is right below the head and throat structure.

Handle and grip

To make you feel as comfortable as you can, your hook should have a nice grip and handle where you can rest your fingers. The grip is where you place your thumb, and the handle is where you place the rest of your fingers. If the grip is too long and bumpy, it will not feel comfortable, and you will have problem crocheting. A bad handle can cause pain in your wrists, which may progress over time.

Materials

It is important to note what kind of material the hook is made out of. It ranges from aluminum, plastic, glass, steel, etc. The hooks material depends upon the yarn you're working with. If you're working with a slippery yarn such as silk, it would be best to use a wooden hook instead of a glass or plastic so it might not slip easily.

What hook does?

As a beginner, you should start with a basic set of hooks. Other types are used for special pattern making and techniques, and it's better to not spend any penny on them until you have basic skills set into as second nature.

Basic hooks

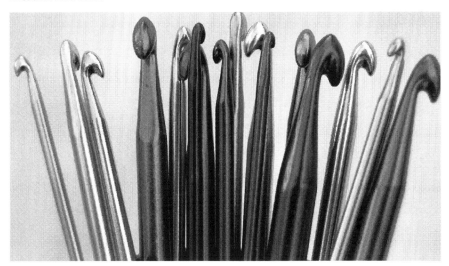

You can buy these individually or in a set of different sizes. The set can be bought at any craft store or online. The sizes are denoted by numbers and/or letters. On average, hooks sizes range from about 5mm to 7.5mm. They are also mentioned as E-J, where E is the shortest, and J is the longest. It is better to buy it as a set rather than picking one individually. These hooks can help you complete your projects with ease if you are a beginner. Different weights of yarns use different length hooks.

Thread hook:

Crochet thread is a very thin and fine string that requires a hook that is also small. Thread crochet hook is smaller than other average hooks and often made out of steel so that it may retain its shape. If you are trying to work with thread crochet, then this hook should be your first choice. As a beginner, you shouldn't work with this yarn because it is difficult, but if you are, use this hook.

Ergonomic hooks:

They are made to provide maximum comfort to your hand. If you are suffering from any hand problems such as arthritis, then this hook is for you. Crochet is a tiring and time-consuming hobby, and if you feel uncomfortable, you will not do a good job. It reduces the pain and stress acting on your wrists.

Tunisian hooks:

Tunisian or afghan crochet hook is used in a specific type of crocheting called Tunisian crochet. It uses different stitching methods and also a different type of hook. It has two heads on each end of the hook.

Light up hooks:

There the same crochet hooks, but the difference is that they have a light in their head so that at night you can see where the stitch is going. This is for people who usually work at night and

do not want to disturb their family.

Yarn Needles

They are a bigger version of regular sewing needles. It is mainly used for weaving at the end of the project. Like hooks, they have different sizes according to yarn's weight. They are mostly made of plastic, but other materials are available. There are a few differences between this and sewing needles:

They are a bit longer than regular sewing needles.

The yarn needles are dull and less sharp than sewing needles.

Mechanism of action is just like sewing needles, so if you know how to sew, then you can work with them as well. They can be replaced by tapestry needles, which look very similar to them.

Scissor

In crocheting, you will need a good pair of scissors to make a smooth working rhythm for yourself. Any type of sewing scissors will do the job if they are sharp enough and have not gone dull. To fulfill all your scissoring needs, it's better just buy a set containing scissors and perhaps some other accessories. Some sewing scissors are listed below:

Dressmaker shears: They look a bit bulky and have sharper cutting edges than normal scissors. The handle is shaped in a way that it is easy to cut cloth on a desk. It is mostly used by tailors and dressmakers hence the name. It is mainly used to cut fabric.

Pinking shears: It is the type of scissor which cuts in a zigzag pattern to give a certain design to the cut. It is used in scrapbooking and making cards. In sewing, it is used to make patterns and hemming. It should only be used on fabrics so that the blades do not get dull.

Office scissors: It is a traditional type of scissors that can be bought in any general store. Its blades match the handle. They don't have anything special to them. They can be used for cutting various items.

Embroidery scissors: They are small scissors that look like something out of a surgeon's box. They are used to make small snips and give a cleaner look to the finished project. It can also be used to cut ribbons and other materials.

Craft scissors: There look like any other general scissor, but it is mainly used for crafting projects. They don't get done quickly

and last for a long time. They are available at any craft store.

Measuring Tape

Every crochet enthusiast should have a measuring tape at hand with them. It is important to make your projects symmetrical and the same length. During your crocheting process, you can't estimate length with your eyes. This will lead to many errors and make your project not look as nice. Measuring in clothing is important, but even when making blankets and tables or dishcloths, to make them look even, you need measuring tape. It's more versatile than using a ruler because you can measure curves with precision with it.

Measuring tape comes in different varieties according to the units they have printed on them. You can get a tape with one side in inches and the other side in centimeters, or you can get a tape with both sides in one unit only. They come in different colors as well, so it's according to your preference which one you want to buy.

Stitch Markers

It is a useful tool in crocheting, and almost all beginners should have them in large numbers so that they can avoid making mistakes. You can crochet without using them, but it will make it more difficult. It is used to mark different sections of the crochet pattern so that you know where a pattern starts and where it finishes. It is also used to keep track of the number of stitches that you have made. If you lose track, then your project might not look good, and symmetry will be lost. You will make a lot of these mistakes, so you will need these to help you as much as possible.

Even more professional crochet users use these stitch markers to keep track of their work. They come in different colors and shapes so you can buy according to your preference. When crocheting big projects for fancy designs, these markers make everything clear and prevent mistakes.

Other Tools You Will Need

There are other tools that you don't need but are preferable that you use them to make your work easier. Here is a list of them below:

Yarn Bowl

It is a bowl that is used to store your yarn when you are knitting your crocheting. The bowl has a little hole at the side of it for the thread to pass through when crocheting. It comes in different stylish designs, and you can use it as a decorative piece as well. It prevents the yarn balls from rolling around your room and stops the thread from coiling up.

Crochet Hook Organizer

When you are crocheting, you are using different hooks of different sizes. To keep all of them organized and ready to use, you would need a crochet hook organizer. It is not ideal for you to let all the hooks lie around. They can get lost or damaged. It will be very convenient for you if they are in one place, you won't need to look around your bag haphazardly. Come in the form of small bags, and there are many styles available for you to choose from.

Row Counter

Many people don't require the use of row counters, but if you trouble to keep the numbers in your head, then this tool might be for you. It helps you to count the number of stitches that you have done. There are two types of row counters available.

A manual row counter increases its number as you press one button, which is, most of the time, the only button. This was used a lot in this modern era; digital row counters have become more popular and have replaced these.

A digital row counter also increases its number as you press a button. It works similarly to a manual row counter and may provide additional processes. Both the manual and the digital counter are similar and price, so it is better to purchase the digital counter.

Blocking Mat

Blocking is a process where you shape your project and give it a nicer look. It removes unnecessary curvature and molds your work in the shape that you want. It works by making your projects a little bit and letting them dry. Blocking isn't always necessary, and it depends upon what kind of project you are working with. The blocking mat provides a surface for your projects to dry on after the dampening process. You can do the blocking process without these mats, but it will make it a lot easier.

Blocking Mats come in various shapes and sizes, and most of them look like puzzle blocks. You can use it for other crafting projects as well.

Holding the Yarn

When you're beginning to crochet, the first thing to learn before even basic stitches is to learn how to hold your yarn and hook properly.

First, you will hold your yarn in your non-dominant hand as you hold any thread.

Next, you will keep your hand straight and flatten it as if it was on a desk.

Now, pass the yarn in between your pinky and ring finger. You can do this using pinky and middle fingers as well. You will do this with your dominant hand.

You can curve your fingers now if that feels natural to you.

Now, the yarn is on top of your hand. You can increase tension by closing your fingers together and decrease it by opening your fingers apart.

Holding the hook

There are many ways to hold your hook. Many crochet enthusiasts fall into one of the two categories, pencil grip, and knife grip.

Pencil grip: If you hold your hook like you would a pencil or a pen, then you fall in this category. The person using pencil grip holds the hook by the thumb, index finger, and middle finger on his or her dominant hand. The hook's motion is from up to down. The person has the same control as he or she does in writing. Sometimes they would hold the thread between the remaining fingers on the dominant hand.

Knife grip: if you hold your hook like you would a dinner knife, then you fall in this category. The person using a knife grip holds by placing their dominant hand above the hook and the index slightly towards the hook's head. The popular belief that it does not give the same amount of control as a pencil grip, but people using knife grip say that it is easier on their hand. The hook's motion is from down to up. These people hold their yarn in the non-dominant hand.

Types of crochet

When we talk about yarn, plenty of people assume yarn is only meant for knitting. Not to mention, many people think knitting and crocheting are the same. Knitting and crocheting have a number of distinctions, especially when it comes to the tools needed to crochet.

Crocheting has its very own finishes, tools, and techniques, and none of this can be achieved through knitting. In Europe, crocheting began to grow in the early nineteenth century, and at that point, it was known as 'shepherd's knitting.' People found this name befitting because crochet seemed like a cheap alternative to purchasing expensive cloth and lace. Queen Victoria also picked up crocheting herself which popularized the craft throughout England.

Crochet is not only historical in this sense, but it was also a lifesaver. They used their skills to create items that eventually helped them earn enough to migrate to America. In the 1900s, Irish folks landed in the US bringing with them their crocheting skills. During the war in the 1950s, crocheting was used for making items such as under-helmet caps and nets for soldiers. It was also used by women to embellish dresses and hats, particularly when they did not have access to money and resources. During the 1960s, it was all the rage for women to have crochet fabric and they began crocheting their own pantsuits and shift dresses.

The rise of crocheting rose in popularity in the 1970s as granny squares made their debut in dresses, jackets, and hooded sweatshirts that were made entirely out of these motifs. Next came the 1980s, and there was a full-blown rise in crochet-use in fashion from crochet cardigans, to fete style toys. Sometime in the 1990s, crocheting dwindled, with the internet and Instagram and other social media platforms, crocheting is back with a modern makeover for all things stylish, from kid's toys to home accessories, to clothing items for both women and men. As beginners, it is also good to know the different types of crochet that exists in our world. Take note that crocheting was not a thing in Europe or America. Different variations existed in different parts of the world to be used for a variety of uses from bags to traditional headgear, clothing, bracelets, adornments, as well as home decor.

Here is a list of 21 well-known crocheting types that still exist in the world and are being practiced everywhere:

1. Amigurumi Crochet

This is the most popular form of crochet, and its country of origin is Japan. Amigurumi refers to the art of creating small, stuffed toys or objects from crocheted yarn. Ami means to crochet or even to knit, whereas nuigurumi refers to stuffed dolls. Whenever you see a doll or toy made of yarn, it is most

likely amigurumi. Many popular culture items have been used to make amigurumi such as Hello Kitty, Mario Brothers, Pokémon, and Winnie the Pooh.

2. Aran Crochet

This type of crochet is usually cabled or ribbed. It has its roots in Celtic culture and features interlocking cables. It is often the choice of crochet used for making bigger items such as scarves, sweaters, and beanies. If you see the word 'Aran' in your patterns, be careful because Aran is also used to describe the weight of yarn. Cozy blankets and throws are usually made using Aran crochet.

Items made using Aran crochet:

Blankets

Jackets

Coats

Scarves

Throws

3. Bavarian crochet

This Bavarian type of crochet is a vintage crochet stitch, and it is traditionally used in rounds. The resulting piece is often a thick fabric that procures for smooth and blended color changes compared to sharp color changes such as the ones commonly seen in a granny square. With Bavarian crochet, you will work in two parts. The first part is the base of clusters whereas the second part is followed by a row of shells. The Bavarian crochet is the fancier cousin to the granny square.

Items made using Bavarian crochet:

Blankets

Shawls

Tabletop covers

4. Bosnian Crochet

This type of crochet has a knit-like fabric and is quite dense in nature. It is crocheted using a slip stitch and crocheted in different parts from the row before. Bosnian crochet also uses a different type of hook, conveniently called Bosnian crochet hook which you can buy, but using regular hooks can work just as well. This type of crochet is called Shepherd's knitting since it also looks like knitted fabrics.

Items made using Bosnian crochet:

Scarves

Beanies

Socks

Hand gloves

5. Bullion Crochet

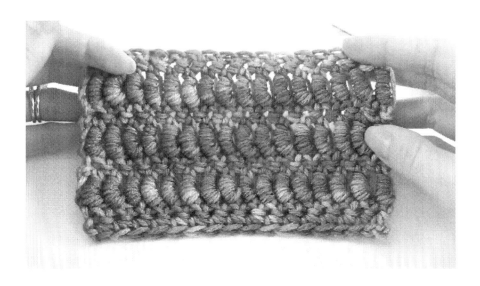

This crochet is a specialized stitch and is achieved using a combination of multiple yarn wraps on a long crochet hook. The result is a distinctive roll stitch that appears quite unique too. Motifs are usually made using bullion crochet, and it results in a uniform, thick, and round motif style piece.

Items made using Bullion crochet:

Stiff items such as placemats

Motifs for decoration

6. Broomstick Crochet

Also known as jiffy lace, broomstick crochet is a type of vintage crochet stitch, which is made with a traditional crochet hook. The resulting stitches are formed around a long and wide object such as broomstick handle, which is how it gets its name. Modern people who crochet use larger crochet hooks or even thick dowels when doing broomstick crochet. This type of crochet is an excellent skill to learn and master as its final product is very beautiful and unique.

Items made using Broomstick crochet:

Delicate shawls

Throw blankets for decoration

7. Bruges Crochet

Ribbons of crochet can be created using Bruges crochet. These ribbons are then crocheted together, and the results show an intricate lace pattern. This is also the most common type of crochet used in home decor items.

Items made using Bruges crochet:

Intricate shawls

Embellishments for clothing

Tablemats

8. Clothesline Crochet

In this crochet style, traditional crochet stitches are done over a clothesline or thick rope or even thick twine to make baskets, and circular mats to hold their shape. This type of crocheting can be traced back to Africa and Nepal.

Items made using clothesline crochet:

Baskets

Mats

Structural wall hanging

9. Clones Lace Crochet

This type of crochet is associated with the Irish lace crochet. It was created to be an alternative to the Irish lace crochet because it's easier and quicker to make than the Irish needlepoint lace. The clones knot used for this type of crocheting requires a unique crochet skillset. Clones lace is a very practical crochet style, and it was commonly used during wars since it was quick and fast to make.

Items made using clones lace crochet:

Open weave scarves

Delicate dresses and tops

10. Cro-hook Crochet

This uniquely named crochet is created using a double-ended hook to create double-sided crochet. This enables you to make stitches on or off at either end of the crochet piece, and this piece does not have a wrong or right side to work on. Because of its nature, this type of crochet is called the Cro-hook or the Cro-knit. This type of crochet closely resembles the Tunisian crochet and is an excellent option if you're working with colors that aren't manageable with other types of crochet.

Items made using clones lace crochet:

Washcloths

Scarves

Baby blankets

11. Filet Crochet

This style is created using chain rows and double crochet stitches. What you get is a grid-like pattern wherein the squares are either filled or not filled, and the negative space is usually there to create images with the pieces. The wonderful thing about this type of crochet is that you can go full-on creative and embed images using empty or full squares of fabric.

Items made using filet crochet:

Baby blankets

Jackets and kimonos

Handbags

Cushions

12. Finger Crochet

This type of crochet is called as such because it does not require hooks. It is similar to finger knitting. It's basically hand fabric which you can use to weave crochet stitches. This is a fun crochet to do when you are a beginner, but the resulting piece has loose tension which is probably why people move on to hooks to make more versatile projects.

Items made using finger crochet:

Simple string bags

Basic scarves

13. Freeform Crochet

This type of crochet is called freeform because there is no pattern or plan to follow. It is entirely up to the person crocheting to create something. This type of crochet is very artistic and organic, making it an excellent option for beginners. However, if you find yourself struggling without instructions or even a plan, then it's best to avoid freeform and follow crochet pieces with patterns.

Items made using freeform crochet:

One-off clothing items

Art pieces

14. Hairpin Crochet

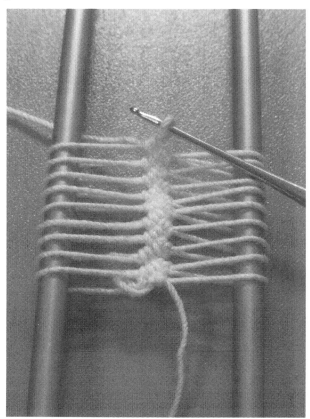

Like the broomstick crochet, the hairpin crochet is made using the traditional crochet hook, but instead of a broomstick, the piece is held taut using thin metal rods. In earlier times, this technique used actual hairpins which is how it got its name. The resulting piece is unique and beautiful.

Items made using hairpin crochet:

Delicate scarves

Shawls

Wraps

15. Micro Crochet

The micro crochet is a modern crochet style and is made using very fine yarn thread with extremely fine or small crochet hooks. It is a very delicate crocheting process and is great for those who are patient and like dainty and small things.

Item made using micro crochet:

Tiny things for dollhouses

Embellishments

Talisman

16. Overlay Crochet

This technique is also quite unique where a base of crochet stitches is made, and then other stitches are added to the top to create a raised pattern. This crocheting technique is more advanced, and it brings many possibilities for you to create intricate pieces.

Items made using overlay crochet:

Potholders

Wall hangings

Handbags

17. Pineapple Crochet

The pineapple crochet is considered more of a general stitch and shape rather than a technique. You can use this crochet to create scarves, doilies, and certain types of clothing. This stitch was very popular in the 1970s, and once you know how to spot this type of stitch, you will see it everywhere.

Items made using pineapple crochet:

Dresses

Tops

Shawls

Wraps

18. Stained Glass Crochet

The stained-glass crochet could be mistaken for the overlay crochet. However, it is different because the top part is normally made using only black yarn to accentuate the colors and create a stained-glass effect. What you get is a very striking crochet pattern.

Items made using stained glass crochet:

Thick, sturdy items

Winter scarves

Handbags

19. Symbol crochet

The symbol crochet is another type of popular crochet and is a favorite among the Japanese. It is also known as the "chart" crochet and is another one of those crochet skills that are crucial to learn because you can make any projects from any crochet books in any language and create them all by looking at a chart.

Items made using symbol crochet:

Complicated patterns that are difficult to explain in words

Intricate designs

Motifs

Foreign language patterns

20. Tapestry Crochet

As the name goes, plenty of color goes into creating this piece, and it is also known as "intarsia" crochet. Tapestry crochet is used in many different parts of the world, and it also has many different methods which result in a variety of styles. If you want to do colorwork, using tapestry crochet enables you to create intricate patterns with a variety of colored yarn.

Items made using tapestry crochet:

Color workpieces

Imagery based designs

21. Tunisian Crochet

This type of crochet is done on a long hook that has a stopper at the end. When you look at Tunisian crochet, it can be very similar to knitting because of the many live loops, and you need to work your loops on and off your hook, similar to knitting.

Items made using tapestry crochet:

Knit-look items

Blankets

Scarves

Learn the Basic Steps by Step

Wherever you look, whoever you ask about starting your crochet career, the answer will be the same — the very base of your crochet is the chain and almost every crochet pattern begins with a chain. If working in rounds or working granny squares, you need to make five chains in a row and join them so that you create a circle. All subsequent squares will be worked in that circle to start shaping your crochet.

How do you create a chain? First you must form a slip knot. In most crochet projects, the first step is making the slip knot. Again, when it comes to slip knots, there are many ways to create it. We will examine one of the easiest ways. First, twist a loose loop of yarn onto the hook. Hold the tail of the yarn between your thumb and index finger. Use the rest of your fingers to control the yarn that keeps unwinding from the ball. Draw the yarn into the loop with your crochet hook. Tighten the loose slip knot that is now on your hook. Remember not to tighten it too much. Make sure your crochet hook can move easily in the loop. Now, start the chain to make progress.

You have your slip knot with a hook, now wrap the yarn over the loop and pull it through to make a new loop. You have made your first chain stitch. In order to make more chain stitches, make another loop and draw the yarn through. You can repeat this as much is needed for your project.

When you have five chains, you can join them to form a circle. As we said before, all the stitches will be worked in that circle. Once the chain is done, you need to join the circle. This is done by putting the crochet hook through the first stitch, the wool around the hook, and pulling it through. This leaves you ready to commence with the first row.

There is no point in changing colors at this stage. You are doing your first chain, your first circle. It's better to try more difficult experiments with color later. But if you really want to change colors, you must cut the wool and pull it through the final loop so that it is tightly fastened. However, by following the guide

step by step with the stitches, you'll need to keep the wool attached, so you will not be able to change colors.

Now you learned the basics — holding your crochet hook and making a chain and a circle to work with. You can increase the number of chains as much as you want to make a larger circle if you want to or need to. When working on a flat item, opposed to one that is worked in rounds, you will need to work across instead of into a circle, thus building your crochet work. How to make a sweater? Merely continue by adding rows, keeping the sides as straight as possible until shaping is required.

Basic Crochet Stitches for Beginners

Having learned how to make a chain, now it's important to understand that the chain is not used only as casting on, but it is also used to create shapes or the corners for granny squares. By the end of this guide, you will have learned how to use chains for those purposes. Now we will take a deep look into the ways to create different stitches and the most common stitches in crochet, giving you the ability to work from patterns.

Single Crochet

The single crochet is the most found stitch and the easiest to make. Easy and fast, it is good for creating shaped items like jackets or skirts. It is also good for decorating finished work as it creates a tight and dense fabric. You can use this stitch alone

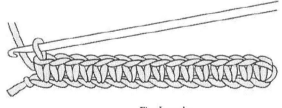

Final result

repeatedly or together with other stitches. It is the most fundamental of all stitches.

How to do it?

Step one. First, prepare a series of chains, then insert your hook on the SECOND chain facing you and your yarn.

Step two. Wrap the yarn towards you with your hook hand. Remember to wrap it from back to front (wrap the yarn from the back to the front — this is called "yarn over" or YO). At this point, pull the hook. If all have been done properly, you are supposed to have two loops to work with.

Step three. Pass the yarn through the two loops. You've completed your first single crochet. Repeat the operation until you finish all the chains. To continue, put your hook onto the next chain stitch and repeat all the operations from step two to complete the second stitch and so on.

We were talking about chain circles before. We can practice the single crochet stitch with the circle. Place the crochet hook into the circle. Put the wool over the hook. Place the wool around and pull it through the two loops on your hook (we went through this before) to form a single crochet stitch. Carry on repeating the same process until you have worked all the circle. When you get to the other side of the circle, join the circle up by placing the hook through the first single crochet that you made, wrap the wool over the hook, and pull through both stitches on the hook. To tie off, cut off the wool and then pull it through the loop on your hook. This time pull tight to fasten.

Double Crochet

The double crochet is the second basic stitch that you need to learn. It is one of the most useful, if not the ultimate useful stitch in crocheting. Once you have mastered it, you can put it to use in creating sweaters, shawls, afghans, home and celebrations décor, and lots of other projects.

We start with our already worked circle.

Insert your hook into the desired stitch. Yarn over your hook (YA) and rotate the hook towards you. With the wrapped yarn, pull the hook through the stitch. At this point, you should have two (2) loops on the hook. YA again and draw the hook with the wrapped yarn into both loops on your hook.

You have now created one (1) double crochet (U.K. style). If all is OK, there should be one (1) unstitched loop on the hook. Repeat.

The double crochet is explained in different ways by different experts from different countries. More than often, there are differences even between experts from the same country. It is such a basic stitch that it cannot have a single description of how to make it. It is always better to hear different opinions to understand properly.

For example, double stitches can be explained as below from a USA expert:

"Start a new chain and join it so you are ready to try a new stitch. The double is a stitch that is a little larger than single crochet. Place the hook into a circle and wind wool around the hook for the commencement of the next stitch. Repeat the stitch outlined in bold above until you have a complete circle then join off the circle as before."

Two ways to explain the same thing — the fun is to find what matches you.

Treble Crochet

Continuing our journey through the main stitches, it is time to learn the treble crochet. Treble crochet is another key basic stitch that you are likely to need for several crochet projects. Trebles can either stand alone, or, like all other basic stitches, can be fused with other ones to make stitch patterns that are pleasing. Trebles are versatile and can be used in every way imaginable. They also work in numerous configurations, such as triangles, circles, squares, rows, and many other shapes. You can use them in almost any thread or yarn, which means you can try practically any material. No need to say that new material must be experimented in a later stage of your learning experience.

You can begin your crocheting from a starting chain. Alternatively, there are many ways you can get started. We will consider the start of our work from a chain for now.

Instructions:

Your chain should be 3 more chains than the number of triple stitches the pattern needs.

Skip the first 4 chains — they are turning chains. Your hook is already through the single loop you have in your chain. YA twice. Insert the hook from the front to the back of the work into the center of the fifth chain (having skipped four, remember?). YO through the chain. You should have four loops on your hook now (see image below).

YO and draw it through the two loops currently on the hook (3 loops still on the hook). YO and draw it through two loops on hook (2 loops remaining on hook). Yarn over, draw yarn

One treble crochet

through the remaining loops on the hook and you've completed one triple crochet (see image below).

YO twice, insert the hook into the middle of the next stitch, YO, and draw it through the stitch (YO, draw through hoops on hook) 3 times. Repeat until you get to the end of the chain. Now you are ready to begin the second row.

To begin, you must turn your work. Start by chaining four (turning chain). Skip the first treble (we talked about it in the beginning). YO twice. On the next triple crochet, insert the hook from the front to the back under the top 2 loops and repeat 3 times. You have now done your first triple crochet. Repeat this step in each treble until you reach the end.

The image below shows what your work should look like when you are working on a flat item rather than a rounded one.

Treble crochet

Using Different Stitches to Their Best Advantages

The best way to get accustomed to the different stitches you have learned is to make a sampler. You can begin with a chain of whatever length you like. The most common and more typical are chains of 25 links for a small sample, but it is totally up to you.

Create a chain and then work one row of double crochet stitches. Turn the work around and work another row of double crochet stitch, then trebles for two rows. Follow this by working into every third hole and creating three trebles into one hole before working on the next third hole to make your next group of trebles. Trebles are very suitable for grouping work. You can try different block groupings.

Do two rows for all the designs that you decide to experiment with. This provides you with a clearer image of what you can produce using that stitch. You can always refer to your sampler when you are making something if you need to verify how you achieved something. Most experts create samplers in multi-

Typical sampler

colored wool so they can clearly see the stitches. It takes a little longer, but it's worth the time.

Decreasing and Increasing

When you make a garment, you will need to decrease and increase to make the shape of the pieces that form the garment. As usual in crochet, what you must do is much easier than you might imagine.

To increase a crochet, just increase the stitches in the same hole, which makes the current row have more stitches than the last.

Decreasing is done by working as shown in the diagram below. The image is better than the description. However, it is worth it to spend some time describing how to decrease.

To decrease in crochet, you the pattern normally but omit the last part of the stitch, leaving the worked loops on your hook. You then work the next stitch as usual, with the last stitch's loop still on your hook. In the end, you pull your hook through all the loops to combine them together.

Although you might consider the above as very complex, it isn't. Like most of the other stitches, it is easier to do it than to explain

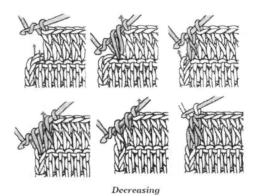

Decreasing

how to do it.

Patterns and Explanation

Single crochet

Single crochet is the least mentioning crochet join to learn and the one that crochets utilize most of the time, either in isolation or in the mix in with different lines. Take as a great deal of time as is required and comprehend how to single crochet confidently by rehearsing the line, considering the way that once you become proficient in single crochet the taller lines will be altogether less unpredictable to master. Single crochet join makes a thick surface that is appropriate for specific sorts of pieces of clothing and extra. It is in like the way the join utilized for toys and compartments since it will, by and large, be worked unfalteringly to plot a solid, firm material that holds up well.

Make an established chain of the fundamental length. Supplement the catch as the second progressed join from the catch and overlay the yarn over the catch, following the huge shock. (You can embed the catch under a couple of strands of the chain, in any case working under only one float, as appeared here, is commonly simple.) Holding the base of the chain firmly with your left hand and tensioning the yarn, arrange afloat back through the chain, as appeared by the monstrous shock. Yarn, and from that point weave in remarkable nuances.

Top of first finished single crochet there are by and by 2 circles on the catch. Next, as appeared by the monster shock. Draw a drift through the two circles on the catch in one smooth activity. As you utilize the yarn, award it to flow through the fingers of your left hand while as of not long ago tensioning it cautiously. Skipped chain at the start of establishment push this finishes the first single crochet. The skipped chain around the start of this first push doesn't consider a join disengaged (at the day's end, it isn't checked when you fuse what number of lines are in the fragment and it isn't worked into in the going with the area).

Urgent stitches

Proceed over the establishment chain, working one single crochet into each chain correspondingly. Around the culmination of the area, turn your crochet to mastermind the yarn at the correct edge of the bit of crochet, orchestrated to start the following line. 1-chain turning chain doesn't consider the first join of line supplement get under the two strands of top of join to start the subsequent fragment, cause one chain to attach. This chain is known as the turning chain, and it brings the work up to the stature of the single crochet join that will follow.

Work the first single crochet into the most raised reason for the first partake in the line underneath. Make a point to embed the catch under the two legs of the "V" of the join. Work particular crochet into the most raised reason for the entirety of the staying single crochets in the line underneath. Near the fulfillment of the line, work the last join into the most critical reason for the last single crochet of the fragment underneath. Work following fragments concerning the resulting line.

Right when you've finished crocheting, cut the yarn, leaving a long, lingering subtlety of at least 6 in (15 cm) long. Remove the catch from the rest of the circle, pass the yarn end through the circle, and pull firmly to close it. Affixing off like this is done in like way.

Half twofold crochet

After single crochet, half twofold crochet comes next arranged by fastening statures. It is firm like single crochet and is likewise genuinely thick, however half twofold crochet creates a somewhat gentler surface, which makes it perfect for warm child articles of clothing. The surface is additionally more intriguing than single crochet, yet not very frilly. Just figure out how to make half pairs once you can make single crochet join with confidence.

Working in columns: Half twofold crochet worked in lines, as here, appears to be identical on the two sides, making it a reversible texture, much the same as every single fundamental join worked in lines. Make an established chain of the necessary length. To start the first, fasten, fold the yarn over the snare. Supplement the snare through the third chain from the snare, once more (as appeared by the enormous bolt) and step a circle back through the chain.

Finished half twofold crochet 2 skipped chains at the start of the column there are presently 3 circles on the snare and draw a circle through every one of the 3 circles on the snare, as appeared by the huge bolt. (This movement turns out to be more fluid with training.)

Work one half twofold crochet into each chain in a similar way. Make sure to begin every half twofold by folding the yarn over the snare before embeddings it through the chain. After working a half twofold crochet into the last chain, turn the work to situate the yarn at the correct edge of the bit of crochet prepared to start the subsequent column. Start the subsequent column by making 2 chains. This turning tie brings the work up to the tallness of the half copies that follow.

Supplement snare under the two strands of top of fastens Leave an end at any rate 6in (15cm) long, so it tends to be darned in later You and work the first half twofold into the highest point of the second join in the line underneath.

Top of chain from past line works a half twofold into every one of the staying half twofold crochets in the line beneath. Work the accompanying lines concerning the subsequent line.

At the point when the crochet is finished, cut the yarn. Expel the snare from the rest of the circle, pass the yarn end through the circle, and pull firmly to shut the circle and attach off safely.

Strategy two: This technique is reasonable for straightforward stripes old yarn starts of a line, if conceivable. Essentially drop the old yarn and get the new yarn through the circle on the snare, at that point start the line in a typical manner. Darn in the yarn tails later.

New slip tie old yarn the two stripes and strong crochet textures. To begin with, affix off the old yarn. At that point place a slipknot on the snare, embed the snare through the first join of the column and draw a circle through the highest point of the line and the circle on the snare.

Stripes worked in essential join offer more potential for imagination than most crochets figure it out. The main procedures you have to learn are the way and when changing hues to change hues to begin another stripe and how to convey the yarns up the side edge of the crochet. Conveying hues upside edge work the last of line with next stripe shading drop old shading at side edge when working stripes in any fasten, consistently change to the next shading on the last of the last column before the following stripe shading is begun.

New shading will shape the first chain of next column drawing through the last of the column finishes the last line. The new shading is presently on the snare prepared to begin the following stripe on the following line; this is so that the first turning chain in the following stripe is in the right shading.

Toward the start of consistently push, wrap stripe shading not being used around working yarn wrapping yarn: If shading isn't required for multiple columns, fold it over the other shading to make sure about it. If it isn't required for more than 8 columns, cut it off and re-join it later.

Twofold crochet

Twofold crochet creates a more open and milder crochet texture than the denser single and half twofold crochet lines. Since twofold crochet is a tall fasten, the texture develops rapidly as you continue, which makes it the most well-known of all crochet join.

Working in lines: As you work twofold crochet in columns, you will see that it seems to be indistinguishable on the front and the back. Make an established chain of any length to rehearse copies, make the same number of chains as required. To start the first, fasten, fold the yarn over the snare.

Addition the snare through the fourth chain from the snare, once more (as appeared by the enormous bolt), and move a circle back through the chain.

There are currently 3 circles on the snare and draw a circle through the first 2 circles on the snare. There are currently 2 circles left on the snare and draw a circle through the staying 2 circles. This finishes the first twofold. In twofold crochet, the 3 skipped chains toward the start of the chain consider the first join of the establishment push. Work one twofold crochet into each chain similarly. Make sure to begin each join with a before embeddings the snare through the chain. After the last fasten of the column has been finished, turn the work to situate the yarn at the correct edge of the bit of crochet prepared to start the subsequent line.

To start the second column of twofold crochet, make 3 chain lines. This brings the work up to the stature of this tall join. Addition snare under the two strands of top of second join top of the first line, at that point, avoiding the highest point of the first twofold in the line beneath, work the first twofold into the highest point of the subsequent fasten. Work a twofold into each line, working the last line into the highest point of the 3 chains. Work the accompanying columns similarly.

Checking single crochet join: With the front of the last line confronting, tally the highest point of each fastening. If you are losing lines as your crochet develops, at that point you are most likely neglecting to work into the last fasten in the line underneath; if you are picking up lines, you may have worked twice into a similar line.

Tallying duplicates: With the front of the last line confronting, consider the turning chain the first line, at that point tally the highest point of each twofold. If you are losing join as your crochet develops, you are likely neglecting to work into the highest point of the turning chain; on the off chance that you are picking up fastens, you might be working into the first twofold of the line, rather than skipping it. Utilizing and a la mode yarn in a cutting-edge colorway, this straightforward however effective twofold line pad adds a bit of style to any room and can without much of a stretch be finished by a learner with negligible sewing aptitudes.

Treble crochet:

Worked in a fundamentally the same as approach to twofold crochet, treble crochet join is roughly one chain length taller because the line is started by folding the yarn over the snare twice rather than just a single time. Trebles are frequently utilized in trim crochet and crochet emblems, and in other fine crochet designs that require an open-finished outcome.

Treble join: Producing a twofold sided texture, either side can be utilized as the correct side. The line worked in columns develops rapidly because the lines are taller yet not excessively much slower to work.

Make an establishment chain, at that point fold the yarn twice over the snare and embed the snare through the fifth chain and draw a circle through the chain. There are presently 4 circles draw a circle through the first 2 circles on the snare. Finished treble crochet 4 skipped chains at starting consider first fasten of line. There are presently 3 circles remaining and draw a circle through the first 2 circles on the snare.

2 circles are remaining and draw a circle through these 2 circles. This finishes the first treble. Concerning all tall crochet join, the skipped chain fastens toward the start of the establishment chain consider the first line of the establishment push. Top of first-line work one treble into each chain similarly. At that point turn the crochet and start the second line with a 4-chain turning chain.

Avoid the highest point of the first treble in the line underneath and work the first treble into the highest point of the second fasten. Work a treble into every one of the rests of the trebles in the line underneath. Work the last line of the column into the highest point of the 4 chains. Work the following columns concerning the subsequent line.

Join taller than trebles are worked similarly as trebles, then again, the yarn is folded over the snare more occasions before the line is started and they require taller turning chains. When you can work twofold trebles effectively, you will likewise have the option to work triple and fourfold trebles absent a lot of exertion. The twofold treble crochet is a valuable expansion to your crochet collection.

Twofold treble line: Worked in columns, twofold treble crochet appears to be identical on the two sides of the texture. Notice how breezy the crocheted surface becomes as the essential fastens get taller. Fold the yarn multiple times over the snare, what's more, embed the snare through the 6th fasten from the snare. Work for the circles free two at once concerning trebles. Make sure to wrap the yarn multiple times around the snare before beginning each join. Begin the following columns with 5 chains.

Triple treble crochet

This line works similarly as twofold treble, then again, actually, the yarn is twisted around the snare multiple times, and the guide is then embedded into the seventh fasten from the snare.

The circles are then worked off two at once, and the following columns start with 6 chains. Fasten statures every one of the following joins gets taller logically and is worked by folding the yarn over the snare again than the past fasten, before embeddings the snare.

Triple treble fastens: This line is perceptibly taller than twofold treble and appears to be identical on the two sides.

When you realize how to function the twofold treble line, you can start to perceive how each after the join is functioned. In this way, as a twofold treble fold the yarn over the snare twice, so a triple treble folds the yarn over your work the circles free similarly as the treble and twofold treble, two by two until there is just the working circle left. Since you know the example, you can make a fast as tall as you can imagine.

Twofold crochet increments

This builds one line toward the finish of the column.

End of the column: Increases on an article of clothing pieces made utilizing twofold crochet and worked utilizing indistinguishable methods from single crochet. Once more, these increments are most now and again filled in as "combined builds" one line is expanded at each finish of the column. First, dc worked into the first dc in push underneath rather than skipping it

Finished first dc worked into the top of turning chain 2 dc worked into the same chain to build one fasten toward the start of a column of twofold crochet, first work the turning chain, at that point work 1 dc into the first dc in the column underneath. Since the first twofold in the column beneath is typically missed, this makes an expansion toward the start of the line. Proceed over the line, working 1 dc into every dc in the standard way. Toward the finish of the line, work 1 dc into the highest point of the turning chain in the column beneath in the standard way. At that point work a second dc into a similar turning chain.

This finishes the one fastens increment toward the finish of the line, as appeared. 1-ch turning chain Increments are additionally much of the time worked in crochet with the goal that they structure little strides at the edge. For instance, to include a 3-join step increment toward the start of a column of single crochet, start by making 4 chains as appeared here.

Step increment at the end of column Works the first Sc into the second chain from the snare. At that point work 1 Sc into every one of them staying 2 chains. This makes a 3-sc increment toward the start of the line. Proceed with the column in the standard way, working 1 Sc into each Sc in the column underneath. Any number of lines can be included thusly and a similar method can be utilized for taller fastens.

Separate length of yarn (appeared here in a differentiating shading for lucidity) Broaden circle so it won't unwind before beginning the line with the progression increment toward the end, expel the snare from the circle toward the start of the column. At that point, utilizing a short length of coordinating yarn, place a slipknot on an extra snare and attract this circle through the last line the column. There is presently one circle on the snare of this structure, the first additional chain toward the finish of the line. Keep causing binds until you have made the same number of as the necessary number of additional fastens.

For a 3-line step increment, make a sum of 3 chains. At that point attach off. Come back to the start of the line, slip the circle back onto the snare and fix it, at that point work as far as possible of the line in a typical manner until you arrive at the additional chains. Work 1 Sc into every one of the 3 included chains. This makes a 3-sc increment. Any number of joins can be included along these lines and a similar method can be utilized for taller lines.

Easy Crochet Pattern for Beginner's

Rainbow Fold-Over Coin Purse

Easy, simple, and eye catching—talk about aesthetical and functional. Have fun making this in rainbow shades, gradient

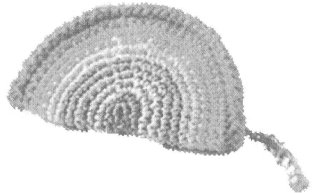

shades, or alternate between your favorite colors.

Note: This works well with any kind of yarn, just make sure you use the appropriate hook according to the yarn's thickness.

1st Round

1. Make a Magic Ring.

2. Make 3 Chains and 12 DCs into the Magic Ring.

3. Slip stitch into the 1st stitch you made and fasten off. You should have 13 stitches in total.

2nd Round

Change yarn color.

1. Make a DC into one of the stitches from the previous row. Pass in a 2nd DC into the same stitch.

2. Finish this round by making 2 DCs in each stitch from the previous round.

3. Slip stitch into the 1st stitch you made and fasten off. You should have 26 DCs in total.

3rd Round

Change yarn color.

1. Start with 1 DC into any stitch from the previous round.

2. In the next stitch, make 2 DCs into the same stitch, and make 1 DC in the next stitch.

3. Repeat step 2 until you finish this round, alternating between 2 DCs and 1 DC.

4. Slip stitch into your 1st stitch and fasten off. You should have 39 DCs.

4th Round

Change yarn color.

1. Make two DCs in two separate stitches.

2. Make 2 DCs into one stitch.

3. Repeat steps 1 and 2 until you finish this round, alternating between 2 DCs in two separate stitches and one 2 DCs in the same stitch.

4. Slip stitch into the 1st stitch you made and fasten off. You should have 52 DCs.

5th Round

Change yarn color.

1. In this round, make 3 DCs in three separate stitches, and stitch in 2 DCs into the 4th stitch.

2. Keep alternating between 3 DCs in three separate stitches, and stitch in 2 DCs into the 4th stitch

3. Slipstitch into the first stitch you made and fasten off. You should have 65 DCs.

6th Round

Change yarn color.

1. In this round, make 4 DCs in three separate stitches, and stitch in 2 DCs into the 5th stitch.

2. Keep alternating between 4 DCs in three separate stitches, and stitch in 2 DCs into the 5th stitch

3. Slipstitch into the first stitch you made and fasten off. You should have 78 DCs.

7th Round

Change yarn color.

1. In this round, make 5 DCs in three separate stitches, and stitch in 2 DCs into the 6th stitch.

2. Keep alternating between 5 DCs in three separate stitches, and stitch in 2 DCs into the 6th stitch

3. Slipstitch into the first stitch you made and fasten off. You should have 91 DCs.

How to Assemble

1. With a needle and thread, sew in a zipper on half of the circle.

2. Fold over, and sew in the other half onto the other side of the zipper.

3. Embellish with beads and sequins or leave as is.

African Flower Hexagon

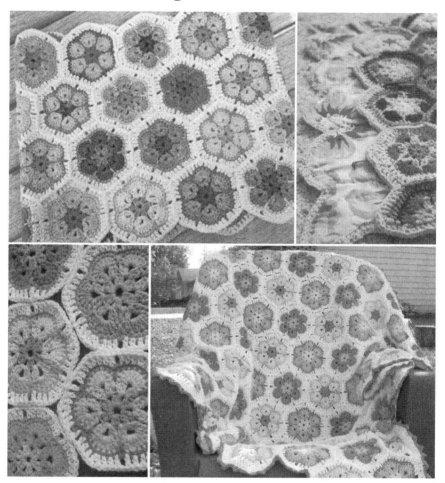

This is one of the most versatile patches you will find in the history of crochet. If you join them together, you can create unique things like stuffed animals, blankets, pillowcases, balls, purses, and so much more. The trick to it is to use random colors to make it brighter and eye catching. This is a good way to make use of scrap yarns.

The pattern is pretty straightforward and easy to do. Connecting it together and experimenting with ideas is what will creativity and style.

Note: This works well with any kind of yarn, just make sure you use the appropriate hook according to the yarn's thickness.

1st Row

1. Start with a Magic Ring.

2. Chain 3 (this will be considered as your 1st DC) and next to it, make a DC, and then a Chain.

3. Make five more sets of 2 DCs and one Chain stitch. You will end up with 6 in total.

4. After your last Chain, slip stitch into your first DC (the 3 Chains).

2nd Row

This will be a good time to change colors.

1. Fasten off into the first Chain to your left.

2. This row will consist of Chain-centered fan stitches. Having said that, Chain 3, DC into the Chain Space, Chain 1, 2 DCs into the same Chain Space. Continue until you have 6 of these around your circle. One set for each Chain from the previous row.

3. End this row by slip stitching into your first stitch.

3rd Row

1. Fasten off into the first Chain to your left.

2. Now create a full fan of 7 DCs. 1st fan should consist of 3 Chain and 6 DCs. Make 6 of these, 1 set for each Chain from the previous row.

3. And like before, end this row with a slip stitch to your first stitch.

4th Row

This will be a good time to change colors again.

1. This row will consist of SCs. Fasten off into the second DC from the previous row.

2. Start making your SCs around the previous row's DCs.

3. When you reach where the fans of the previous row meet, make a long stitch, going through all the way to where the fans from the 2nd row meet.

4. Continue your SCs around the fans, do not forget to make a long stitch where the fans meet.

5. When you've gone all around the flower, slip stitch into your 1st stitch.

5th Row

This is another time to change colors if you please.

1. Make SCs around the flower again, but this time, only in the back loops.

2. Take off from the last stitch you had left off, make 3 SCs, and when you reach the "corner" of the hexagon (which is the 4th stitch from the previous row, in other words, the center of the "petal"), make a Chain before making another SC in the same stitch.

3. Keep making SCs on the back loops of the previous row, remembering that when you reach the center stitch of the "petal" you need to make a Chain, and then make an SC again in the same loop the last stitch was in.

Classic Granny Square

Whether you're a newbie or a pro, every crocheter must know this pattern! This motif is as versatile as the African Flower Hexagon, but this one is a go-to patch for making basic yet beautiful afghans.

Note: This works well with any kind of yarn, just make sure you use the appropriate hook according to the yarn's thickness.

It is important to check tension and maintain even stitches.

1st Row

1. Start with a Magic Ring.

2. Chain 3 and make 2 DC in the Magic Ring.

3. Chain 2, and make 3 DC in the Magic Ring. Repeat 2 more times until you have 4 sets, forming a roundish square.

4. Slip stitch into your 1st stitch. You should have 12 DC stitches in total.

2nd Row

1. Turn your work over and in the Chain Space you made in 1st row, Chain 3, then make 2 DCs.

2. Chain 2 and make 3 DCs in the same Chain Space.

3. Chain 1 and make 3 DC in the next Chain Space.

4. Repeat steps 2 and 3 until you finish the whole row.

5. Slip stitch into your 1st stitch for this row.

3rd Row

1. Turn your work over and Chain 3 and make 2 DCs into the 1st Chain 2 space from the previous row.

2. Chain 2 and make 3 DCs into the same Chain 2 space.

3. Chain 1 and make 3 DCs into the next Chain Space.

4. Repeat step 3 once more, and then repeat step 2.

5. Keep doing steps 3 and 4 until you complete this row. Finish off with a slip stitch.

You can make this Granny Square as big as you prefer, keeping in mind that you need to CH 2 for every "corner" to accommodate a larger amount of stitches, and to also turn it over after every row. Again, maintain the tension so that you will not end up with a deformed Granny Square.

You can then join these squares with a tapestry needle to make an afghan, a bag, a trendy top, and a lot more. Your imagination and creativity will flourish with this easy and versatile motif!

Granny Crochet Blanket

This is a long-term project. It's easy, but it requires a lot of patience and commitment. If you think you're ready to make this gorgeous blanket, then let's get going!

Note: This works well with any kind of yarn, just make sure you use the appropriate hook according to the yarn's thickness. It is important to check tension and maintain even stitches.

Here are some things you need to know before starting this project:

This blanket measures 40in x 69in or 100cm x 175cm

Each Granny Square should measure 3.5in x 3.5in or 9 x 9cm

You need to make 135 Granny Squares for this project.

You need to stitch or crochet together the motifs in 15 rows of 9

Sample steps on how to connect the squares:

1st Round

1. Connect joining yarn with a slip stitch in any corner Chain Space with Chain 3, 2 DCs, Chain 3, and 3 DCs. In the same corner Chain Space, Chain 1

2. Make 3 DCs, and Chain 1 three times, and then make 1 DC in the next corner Chain Space, DC 2 together in the same corner Chain Space and corner Chain Space on next square, and 1 DC in the same corner Chain Space, then Chain 1.

3. Repeat step 2 for each square until you reach the other corner of the blanket.

4. Make 3 DCs, Chain 3, and 3 DCs in the blanket corner Chain Space, Chain 1.

5. Repeat from step 2 to step 4 for each side of the blanket, join with slip stitch in first DC, then fasten off.

2nd Round

1. Connect joining yarn with a slip stitch in any corner Chain Space, Chain 3, 2 DCs, Chain 3, and 3 DCs in the same corner Chain Space, Chain 1.

2. Make 3 DCs and Chain 1 until you reach the next blanket corner Chain Space, make 3 DCs, Chain 3, 3 DCs in blanket corner Chain Space, Chain 1

3. Repeat step 2 for each side of the blanket, join with slips stitch in first DC, and then fasten off.

3rd to 4th Round

1. Repeat 2nd Round.

Maybelle Flower Coasters

Make these vintage crochet flower motifs into gorgeous coasters. Gradient, variegated, solid, or change colors for every row to make these coasters more personalized.

Note: For this pattern, I recommend you use a chunky cotton yarn along with an appropriately sized hook.

1st Round

1. Chain 10 and slip stitch into your 1st stitch to form a circle.

2. Chain 3 this will count as your 1st DC for this round.

3. Make 23 more DCs

4. Then slip stitch into your 1st stitch.

2nd Round

1. Chain 5 then SC into the 3rd stitch from the base of your chain.

2. Repeat step 1 until you finish this row.

3. Slip stitch into the 1st chain you made. You should have 8 half circles in total.

3rd Round

1. Slip stitch into the Chain Space.

2. In the same Chain Space, Chain 3 (this will be your 1st DC) make 1 more DC, Chain 2, 2 more DCs, and 1 Chain.

3. Repeat step 2 into all the Chain Spaces. Change the 1st Chain 3 into 1 DC.

4. Slip stitch into the 1st stitch you made.

4th Round

1. Slip stitch your way into the 1st Chain Space of 2.

2. In the same Chain Space, Chain 3 and make 6 DCs, and 1 SC into the Chain of 1 from the previous round.

3. Make 7 DCs into the Chain Space of 2, and then 1 SC into the next Chain of 1 from the previous round.

4. Repeat step 4 until you've made fan stitches of 7 DCs into each Chain Space of 2.

5. Slip stitch into your 1st stitch, fasten off, and tuck in ends

T-Shirt Yarn Basket

Have you ever worked with T-Shirt yarn before? This will be a great pattern to start off with! Even though this pattern works with any kind of yarn, I suggest you use a T-Shirt yarn.

Note: This works well with any kind of yarn, just make sure you use the appropriate hook according to the yarn's thickness. It is important to check tension and maintain even stitches.

1st Round

1. Start with making 3 Chains and slip stitching into the 1st stitch to make a ring.

2. Make 7 SCs into the ring.

2nd Round

1. SC 2 in each stitch. you should have 14 SCs when you finish this round.

3rd Round

1. Alternate making 1 SC in one stitch, and then 2 SCs in one stitch. you should have 21 SCs when you finish this round

4th Round

1. Alternate making 2 SCs in the next two stitches, 2 SCs in one stitch. You should have 28 SCs when you finish this round.

5th Round

1. Alternate making 3 SCs in the next three stitches, 2 SCs in one stitch. You should have 35 SCs when you finish this round.

6th Round

1. Alternate making 4 SCs in the next four stitches, 2 SCs in one stitch. You should have 42 SCs when you finish this round.

7th Round

1. Alternate making 5 SCs in the next five stitches, 2 SCs in one stitch. You should have 49 SCs when you finish this round.

8th Round

1. Make SCs in the back loops of each stitch. You should have 49 SCs when you finish this round.

9th to 16th Round

1. Make SCs around, maintaining 49 stitches for each round.

17th Round

1. Make 22 SCs then Chain 9 to make a handle, skip 3 stitches, SC in the next 21 stitches.

2. Chain 9 and skip 3 stitches again, to make the second handle.

18th Round

1. Continue making SCs around the rim.

2. When you reach the handles, SC over the stitches, making as many as needed to cover over the stitches from the previous round.

3. Slip stitch, fasten off and tuck in the ends.

Choosing A Crochet Pattern

Mussel Pattern

For this pattern, three or more stitches are crocheted into the same puncture site, forming a triangle that looks like a small shell. On the left and right of the shell, one usually goes over a few stitches to compensate for the increase in stitches by the shells, which turn one stitch into at least three. Shells look best if you crochet them out of chopsticks or double sticks.

In order to crochet a mussel out of three sticks, one works first, where the stitch is to be placed, first a stick, in order to work. Then in the same puncture, place two more sticks. To complete the pattern and the number of stitches in the row, it can sometimes be necessary to crochet half-shells at the beginning and end of the row. To do this, at the beginning of each turn, work two sticks into the corresponding puncture site. At the end of the row, place two sticks in the last stitch.

Tuft Stitches

Tufts are basically nothing but inverted shells. They consist of several stitched-together stitches; these can be fixed stitches but also double or multiple sticks. Not only do they provide a decorative pattern, but they are also often used to remove one or more stitches in a row.

The base of this tuft is spread over several stitches while their heads are gathered in a stitch. To do this, do not crochet the stitches you want to gather at first to pull the thread in one go through all loops on the needle in the last step. How to do it exactly, shows the following instructions for a tuft of three sticks.

1. Work the first stick as usual until there are only two loops on the needle. Do the same with the second stick so that you have a total of three loops on the needle.

2. The third stick is also crocheted up to and including the penultimate step. There are four loops on the needle. Now, get the thread.

3. To complete the tufting, pull the thread through all four loops on the needle.

Burl

Knob stitches are very distinctive and give the crochet a beautiful plastic structure. It is a group of several rods or multiple rods, which are worked in the same puncture site and then blended together, making it a combination of shell and tufts. Pimples are worked in the back row. The following shows how to crochet a knot stitch out of five sticks.

1. Crochet the first stick at the point where you want to create the knit stitch until you have only two loops on the needle.

2. Follow the same procedure for the following four rods working in the same puncture site.

3. Now, there should be a total of six loops on the crochet hook.

4. In the last step, pick up the thread and pull it in one go through all the loops on the needle. It is advisable to secure the knit stitch with a chain stitch (take the thread and pull it once again through the stitch on the needle) so that the stitches remain firmly together at the top and the knobby effect maintains the desired plasticity.

Colorful Pimples

It looks happy when you work the pimples in different colors. In addition, you can meaningfully use small yarn remnants in this way.

To crochet a colored nub, work the last solid stitch in front of the nub in the base color until there are still two loops on the needle to finish the stitch with the yarn for the nub. Then crochet the nub as described in the new color. Use the chain stitch to secure the knob; work again in the basic color, with which you then continue crocheting until the next knob.

Flat Nubs

Flat knobs are made of half-sticks and are slightly less plastic than knobs or the popcorn stitches described below. They are often used to crochet baby clothes and cuddly blankets. They are crocheted according to the same principle as the pimples. It is important that you do not work too hard. The following example illustrates how to crochet a flat knot of three half rods in one go through all the loops on the needle. It is advisable to secure the knit stitch with a chain stitch (take the thread and pull it once again through the stitch on the needle) so that the stitches remain firmly together at the top, and the knobby effect maintains the desired plasticity.

1. First, thread the thread around the needle, then insert it into the loop into which the flat knot should be placed. Get the thread.

2. Repeat this step twice so that there are finally seven loops on the crochet hook. Then you pick the thread and pull it in one go through all the loops.

3. Finally, secure the flat knot with a warp stitch by retrieving the thread and pulling it through the loop on the crochet hook.

Popcorn Stitches

For a popcorn mesh, one works—as well as the knobs or flat knobs—a whole group of stitches in a puncture site. The stitches are not taken off together but individually terminated and bundled in a further step. They create plastic accents in even patterns and can be crocheted from fine yarn, as well as from thicker wool qualities.

1. Crochet a group of five rods in a single injection site when you wanted to crochet a shell. Then slightly lengthen the working loop on the needle by pulling lightly.

2. Now, pull the needle out of the working loop in order to put it into the debarking element (i.e., the mesh V) of the first stick.

3. Then, pick up the working loop and pull it through the second loop on the needle (the debittering stick of the first stick). Secure the stitch with a chain stitch. Pull the thread through the loop again.

Filet or Net Pattern

For this effective but, in principle, quite simple pattern, you crochet from bars and air meshes a grid. You can combine filled and empty boxes in such a way that geometric or floral motifs are created. A simple net pattern without "fillings" can be crocheted very fast. For example, it is good for light scarves and bandages, and if you can handle it with sturdy material works, you would have crocheted, in no time, a shopping net. If you work alternately filled and empty boxes, you can pull a cord through the stitches to close about a bag.

1. Crochet a chain of meshes first. The number of stitches for your basic chain must be divisible by two. In addition, crochet six more pieces of air.

2. Now, for the first box, insert into the sixth stitch of the chain of stitches as seen from the needle and work a chopstick.

3. Crochet an airlock again. For the subsequent chopsticks, pass over a stitch in the sling chain. Then, crochet one

more air mesh and the next chopstick into the next, but one mesh of the basic chain work. So, continue until the end of the series.

4. Start the next row with three first-streaks and one streak with the next-stick link.

5. Now, work a chopstick into the scraping member of the penultimate stick of the previous row, crochet a loop of air, pass one stitch of the previous row, and work another stick into the corresponding chopsticks of the previous row. The last stitch of the row works in the third link of the chain of meshes counted from below.

6. To crochet a filled box, do not join the sticks with an airlock, but crochet between the base sticks other sticks around the air mesh of the previous row. To do this, just stick in the empty box to get the thread.

7. If the box of the previous row is also filled, work the "stuffing stick" into the scraping member of the pre-row filler.

Grid Pattern

A likewise light and transparent pattern is the grid pattern, which is crocheted from air mesh and solid or warp stitches. Experimental minds vary the length of the air-chain chains to work an uneven lattice structure.

Normally, the arcs are one-third longer than the basic piece of the previous series. The arcs in the following instructions are five air mesh long, the base three chains.

1. Work an air chain. The number of stitches should be divisible by four. For this crochet, add two air meshes.

2. Now, anchor the first bow by crocheting it into the sixth stitch of the base with a slit stitch or a sturdy stitch. Then crochet five loops of air, pass three meshes in the basic loop, and anchor the bow in the fourth loop of the air.

3. The last bow of the row is attached in the last loop of the base chain.

4. Now, crochet five air stitches and then a single crochet stitch into the bow, then another five stitches, and then a single crochet stitch into the next bow. The last bow is anchored in the third spiral of the first row.

5. Start the next series again with five air stitches, fasten them with a sturdy stitch in the first loop of air mesh, and work in the grid pattern to the end of the row. The last tight stitch back into the third spiral air mesh of the front row work. Continue working until the desired height is reached.

Crochet Subjects Around an Air-Mesh Bow

In crochet instructions for flowers, for example, one often reads the instruction that a group of stitches, often chopsticks, should be worked into an air-mesh arch. For this, you do not sting into the mesh links of the chain but into the bow so that the chain of mesh is crocheted.

Practical Crocheting Tips

Here are some useful and helpful tips and tricks that will make crocheting simpler and keep you increasingly sorted out.

1. At the point when the afghan you're crocheting turns out to be excessively long and substantial, place stitching rings around the end you've just wrapped up. It's going to make it easy to turn it over just when you crochet the next line.

2. At a point when someone asks you to do something else for them, make notes in a pad of paper. Write their name when they need it, and the thing they need to crochet — in addition, record where the pattern can be found. When you finish the crocheted job, snap a photo of it and keep it in a photograph collection, so when somebody asks what you crochet, you can show it to them.

3. Threading a large eyed needle with the free strings after completing a venture and meshing the loose lines into the undertaking is more straightforward than utilizing the hook. It just takes minutes to do an entire cover with numerous string changes.

4. If you are a beginner and regularly lose your place, write down the patterns on lined paper, each guidance in turn.

5. When traveling, utilize an empty plastic coke bottle to prevent the hooks from getting away.

6. To keep squares perfect as you crochet them before assembling them, keep them in a secured plastic pack. Utilize a little cushion of paper and pen to monitor what number of squares you've made.

7. Prevent skeins and balls from getting tangled by cutting a gap in the highest point of an unfilled plastic espresso holder, at that point softening the edges of the opening with a lighter or match to prevent the fleece from catching. If you have a few activities going on simultaneously, use marks or tape on the tops or sides of every compartment to write the task name and other significant data. Tape a little piece of dryer sheet inside every head to keep the fleece smelling pleasant and forestall static.

8. Utilize a three-ring fastener with clear sheet binders to arrange your patterns. Utilize a pencil pocket likewise with three gaps for additional hooks, measure check, and whatever else you need to keep convenient.

9. At the point when you open another crochet ball of string, take the paper and put it inside the focal point of the ball. At that point, when you need a new series, you'll have the shading and all the data for your next ball of string.

10. Utilize a toothbrush holder to hold your hooks.

11. It's anything but difficult to find, and you can drop hooks in your handbag and go.

12. To store scrap yarn, purchase a reasonable collapsible hamper, put a similar shading yarn in plastic essential food item packs, and save every one of the sacks in the hamper.

13. Take a two-liter plastic jug and slice the center to make an entryway. At that point, place your huge yarn inside and put the string through the neck. It keeps the 8oz yarn sorted out.

14. Make your new hook smooth by rubbing it into your hair.

15. To keep woven-in ends from coming free, weave on an oblique line rather than straight up or over.

16. To maintain the crochet yarn / cotton ball from moving over the floor, put it in a small plastic bag with handles, drape it on your arm, and crochet comfortably.

17. Use a safety pin as a pointer to complete the rounds. It comes off and on effectively and doesn't shred like a piece of yarn markers.

18. Store yarn in a zippered sofa-bed sack.

19. Paperclips make extraordinary stitch counters. Simply pop one on the stitch you need to stamp. Safety pins

work incredibly as well and are somewhat simpler to put on and take off.

20. Utilize a wooden wine rack for yarn stockpiling. It works extraordinary, looks dynamite, and is a pleasant conversation piece.

21. Empty medicine bottles can be convenient for keeping smaller crochet instruments like column counters, dabs, and yarn needles.

Since you're composed, have a ton of fun crocheting!

1. Learn all you can about crochet supplies so you can purchase what suits you.

2. Remove all obstacles in your way. This can be your long hair, jewelry and cats (because they cannot resist a ball of yarn!) so you aren't interrupted while you work.

3. Position the yarn in a place that unwinds easily.

4. Be prepared to switch hooks. Novice crocheters often work too tight or too loose. If this is the case for you, change your hook. (Too tight = a larger hook needed, too loose = a smaller hook needed).

5. Take the time to make gauge switches, practicing all the stitches that you'll need for a pattern.

6. Don't be afraid to experiment with making a project your own. If you make a mistake, you can always unravel the last few stitches.

7. Take a break. If you get frustrated, taking a breather can help you refocus when you come back to work.

8. A break is also good for hand and finger stretching. You don't want to injure yourself as you work, or you might never get to finish your project.

9. Keep up to date with everything crochet. There are plenty of online e-zines and forums filled with all of the latest patterns, tips, tricks and information. You never know what you'll learn!

10. Of course, the best way to master crochet is through practice. After all, practice makes perfect!

Left-Handed Crocheting

Being left-handed needn't stop you from learning to crochet. It may seem challenging at first, after all most patterns are aimed at right-handed users, and attempting to manage these will have you working backward. Below are a few ways to get around this:

1. Reverse the pattern so that you're holding the crochet hook in your right hand. This means that the 'wrong side' of the pattern is actually 'the right side'.

2. Practice holding the hook until you're comfortable. A lot of left-handed crocheters have created their own variation on the 'pencil' or 'knife' hold, in a way that suits them.

3. Learn by sitting across from someone right –handed, mirroring their movements!

Creating Your Own Pattern

You may get to a stage where you have been crocheting for a while, and you'd like to try your hand at creating your own pattern.

To do this, there are a few things you should keep in mind:

- Master all the basic crochet stitches before you start, so you know the appearance and usage of each one.

- Follow a variety of patterns, noticing the mechanics of how they put a project together.

- Learn to count stitches and rows, so you'll be able to work them into your own.

- Experiment as much as you can with materials, tools and ideas.

- Get decorative with your creations. Practice with shapes and styles.

- Try to modify an existing pattern for practice.

- Learn how a gauge works – it's a great way to calculate stitches effectively.

- Sketch what you'd like to create to assist you in the shapes you'll need.

- Start simple and small, building complexity as you get used to it.

- Write everything down as you go, and maybe allow other crocheters to practice your pattern to get a better idea of how it'll work.

The Economic Part of Crocheting

Many people around the world have been able to learn crocheting skills. It is an industry that has grown and has empowered very many men and women around the world. This has greatly improved the economy. Below are some of the economic impacts of crocheting. Do crochets have an economic impact? Several people may not find crocheting beneficial. They may not see it as a source of income, but it contributes immensely to the economy.

During cold seasons people look for warm things to keep them warm. They, therefore, have to purchase scarfs, sweaters, socks and other products made from yarn. This increases the rate of yarn production as a result of the increase in demand for crocheted items. This is said to lead to the growth of the economy. Below are some of the economic impacts brought by crocheting.

So many crocheting companies have been opened which has created employment opportunities for many families around the world. They can take care of their families from the income they earn from the crocheting companies.

Women can crochet items and sell them to people in their neighborhood which enables them to earn some income. This helps to improve the economy since they do not become dependent on the government for their survival. The government is, therefore, able to concentrate on other development projects since its people are not overly dependent on them. This acts as a source of income for the publisher which also helps in the growth of the economy.

The experts in this area have also taken up the role of training more people in crocheting. This ensures the empowerment of more people which means more skilled individuals in a country. Individuals who have specialized in information technology also develop apps which contain crochet instructions. This has helped people to have easy access to the skills so anyone can install the app and learn the skills in their own free time.

Social and Traditional Impact of Crocheting

Crocheting has had a great impact on our society. The skill keeps on being passed on from one generation to another. This has helped a lot in impacting people's lives socially and even traditionally. Below are some social and traditional impacts brought about by crocheting?

For Charity: Most often, we find ourselves with different types of crotchets which we mostly make during our free time. One can craft some items and give them out for charities. It will always feel great when one benefits from an item crocheted with a lot of love. It will act as a way of showing your generosity and sense of care for others. One will feel good when someone appreciates something that was made purposely to suit their need.

Aesthetic value: Crocheting can display the beauty of a tradition. Before the invention of big companies that dealt with the manufacturing of clothes, people used to wear crocheted clothes. Some people make crochets to beautify the environment. One, therefore, makes items that they are sure that they will make their environment calm. This will enable them to feel relaxed whenever they are around.

Boost self-esteem: We all feel good when complimented for doing something so well. Compliments motivate us to produce better crochets which are better than the previous ones. When we sell the crafts, we made or give it as a gift, it boosts your self-esteem. You feel great about your accomplishments. Self-esteem can also be built through learning new skills. One can feel productive which creates beauty through self-expression.

Reduces stress and anxiety: We all get stressed up at some point in our life. We may become anxious as a result of the strenuous activities we may have engaged in on our daily activities. One needs to give themselves a break. Getting a yarn and crochet would be of great help in relaxing their mind. It is through the repetition of the stitches as you count the rows that your mind gets some kind of relaxation. All the anxiety thoughts are set free since your focus is on creatively making the crochets.

Eases and relieves depression: Our emotions keep changing depending on the occasion. For instance, in the grieving period, it seems impossible to overcome your grief. Most times we feel like the world has come to an end. Crocheting can be a comforter during the grieving period. Crafting such as crocheting is said to be helpful in the stimulation of dopamine which enables one to feel happier and emotionally stable.

Keeps one busy: Imagine you are left at home alone. No other work for you, you can choose to do some crocheting. You will be relaxing at the same time keeping yourself busy. You don't have to create wonderful products out of it. The whole idea is to keep your mind engaged through a useful course which may help you earn some income or even contribute to charity. In a scenario where you are following up on a program on the television, your hands will be busy crafting while your eyes are glued to the television. The best thing about crocheting is that one can engage every member of the family. They will be able to contribute to various ideas about what you are making and suggestions on colors and even designs.

Brings communities together: There are many ways to bring people together. One of them is having yarn crafting introduced to a community. They can have a meet up in public to do crocheting. The organizers can organize a fiber fair together with related events. This will be of great help since people from different places will be able to meet and share ideas. They will be able to learn from one another hence more creative designs. The community can even come together and build yarn stores which will benefit the community from the sales made in the store. All the participants can also buy the yarn at a reduced price which will enable them to make more crocheted items for sale. They in return become more productive which brings economic empowerment amongst them.

BONUS Easy and Fun Crochet Patterns for Children

Heart Amigurumi Pattern

There aren't any intricate details, whatsoever, so this project is perfect for absolute beginners. For this pattern, you can use a 2 mm crochet hook, but you may also try with a slightly bigger hook and see what looks better.

To start off, you will make a magic ring and work six single crochet (sc) into the magic ring. Now, if you don't know how to make a magic ring, it is pretty simple.

All you need to do is to make a loop and almost as if you are making a chain pull the yarn to the front and chain one, then stitch sc around the ring, preferably six or seven sc and pull the yarn tail to tighten. All you need to do is secure with a slip stitch and your first round is complete. You also need to weave in the end so that it doesn't unravel.

The reason why amigurumi start with a magic ring is that it doesn't leave a big hole in the center, unlike chaining and creating a ring out of chains. This way, you can tighten the ring as much as you would like. For the second round, you will do six increases by working two sc into each of the sc from the previous round.

For the third round, you will work one sc and an increase in the following. You will repeat this six times, which will result in 18 stitches at the end of the round. In the fourth round, you will crochet sc in an sc stitch and another in the following and then you will work an increase in the third stitch. You will repeat this six times, which will result in 24 stitches at the end of this round. In the fifth round, you will crochet seven sc and then an increase, and repeat it two more times.

At the end of this round, you will have 27 stitches. And then for the next three rounds, sc all the stitches. At the end of the ninth round, you will have 27 stitches. Fasten off the yarn and repeat this whole process for the second 'hump'. Once you have finished the second 'hump', do not fasten off, but join the two

together. You will do this by slip stitching three of the stitches from both of the humps. This way, each of the humps will have 24 available stitches and three connected.

For the second part, you will create the wide part of the heart. You will sc the tenth and eleventh round (48 stitches in total). Then you will begin decreasing. All the patterns will be repeated three times. For the following round, you will work 14 sc and then one decrease.

Repeat these two more times (45 stitches in total). In the following round, you will work 13 sc and then one decrease and again repeat this two more times (42 stitches). As you can see, a pattern arises. For each of the following rounds, you will crochet a certain number of stitches and then make a decrease and then repeat it two more times.

Each time you will decrease the number of stitches for three. It is that simple. In the end you will have six stitches. This is when you're going to insert the stuffing into your heart amigurumi and finish off the project. If you feel that it is finishing abruptly, then make another round of sc once and decrease once, which will leave you with three stitches that can be worked together and then you can fasten off the yarn.

Emoji Amigurumi Pattern

The following pattern is also one of the easier and simpler in terms of crocheting the basis. However, it has some finishing details that may be a bit more complicated for some people; but all in all, I think it is still one of the easiest amigurumi patterns to make. Again, I suggest using a smaller gauge hook, but if you feel like experimenting, please do so and if you are satisfied with the outcome, keep it that way. Essentially, you will be making an amigurumi ball that by adding different finishing details will turn into emoji.

Now, let's get started! To start off, make a magic ring and work six sc into the ring. It would be a good idea to mark the beginning of the round with a different color yarn or a stitch marker, just so that you know whether you have finished a round. In the second round, you will increase in all of the stitches. In the third round, you will work one sc and increase once, and repeat this five more times.

This way, you will increase by six stitches, 18 in total. For the fourth round, crochet two sc and increase once, and repeat this five more times. In the fifth round, you will crochet three sc and increase once and repeat this again five more times. For the final increase, you will crochet four sc and increase once and repeat this five more times. If you want your ball to be bigger, you can continue this way until you reach the desired size. However, we will stop increasing here and sc all the stitches without increasing for the rounds 7-12.

Once we have done the sc for five rounds, we will start decreasing. We will do this by reversing what we previously did. Now, for the 13th round, you will crochet four sc and decrease once and repeat this five more times. In the 14th round, crochet three sc and decrease once and repeat until the end of the round. In the 15th round, crochet two sc and decrease once; repeat five more times. In the 16th round, crochet one sc and decrease once.

For the final round, you will work six decreases, and finish off. But, before that, you will fill the ball with stuffing and then work the final round. Crochet all of the remained stitches together and fasten off the yarn. Of course, if you want, you can make the ball in multiple colors.

Now that you have finished the base, which is the ball, you can work on the details. For eyes, you can crochet simple round motifs. For the wide-open mouth, you can crochet a semicircle, either in rows or rounds. Sew them onto the ball and embroider the black details onto the ball.

You can do this either with an embroidery needle or with a crochet hook. Though if you decide to try with a crochet hook, you may find it a bit difficult and the lines will be thicker. All in all, it is a fun little project and I'm sure that you definitely need one of these. If not for your children, then it is perfect for you. I would use it as an anti-stress ball, wouldn't you?

Jellyfish Amigurumi Pattern

Now that you've completed simple amigurumi projects, it is time to move on to some more complex ones. In terms of difficulty, I would rate this one as a medium, because even though there are more elements to the pattern, it is still pretty easy to make.

You may use a 3.5- or 4-mm hook for this project and a color by your choice. As you can see, these are adorable and I'm sure your kids will love it. You can also make these as key chains if you prefer bulky and gigantic, yet adorable key chains.

So, to start, you will make a magic ring and crochet eight sc into the ring. Now, just like with the previous projects, you can keep track of the round beginnings with some markers and work in spirals, or you can slip stitch at the end of each round, just like you would normally do. It is up to you.

You can try both these techniques and see what suits you the best. So, for the next round, if you are ending the rounds with a slip stitch, you will chain one, which will count as one sc. On the other hand, if you want to work in spirals, you will just continue with an sc. It is up to you, but once you decide, do keep working that way for every round. For the sake of simplifying the pattern, I will not mention slip stitches nor chain one because this will be done in spirals.

In the second round, you will increase for all the stitches by working two sc in each of the stitches from the previous round. By the end of this round, you will have 16 stitches. For the third round, you will crochet a sc in one stitch and increase in the following and you will repeat this until the end of the round, which will result in 24 stitches. For the fourth round, you will crochet sc in each of the following two stitches and then make an increase. You will repeat this until the end of the round, i.e. two sc, one increase. This way, you will have 32 stitches by the end of the round.

For the following round, you will work sc in the next three stitches and increase in the next one. Repeat this throughout. This round will have 40 stitches in total. In the sixth round, you will crochet sc in four stitches and increase in the next one and repeat this throughout.

As you may guess, this round will have 48 stitches in total. For the next two rounds, seventh and eighth, you will sc into each of the stitches from the previous round. In the ninth round, you will work sc into five stitches and an increase in the following one and repeat this until the end of the round. This round will have 56 stitches in total. For the rounds 10-14, you will work sc into all of the stitches.

And for the final 15th round, you will crochet sc into two stitches, then work a decrease by a single crochet two together, then work one sc, and another decrease. You will repeat this throughout the round, i.e. you will work two sc, decrease, one

sc, and decrease. This will result in having 40 stitches at the end of the round. Now, you will fasten off the yarn and weave in the ends.

So, now that we have finished the top part of the jellyfish, we need to make the bottom as well as the tentacles. First, we will make the tentacles. It is very easy and you can make them in a matter of minutes. For the spiral ones, you will need to chain 30-60, whatever is your desired length.

Then work two to three single crochet or half double crochet (hdc) into all of the chains and that's it. Fasten off the yarn, leaving the tail. You can make these in different lengths. Next, you can make the straight ones too. Again, you will chain 30-60, whatever you feel is long enough, though these should be the same length or a bit longer than the spiral ones. Then, you will work sc or hdc in each of the chains and you're done with tentacles. You should make around six of each of the tentacle types.

Next, we will make the bottom part. Just like with the top part, you will make a magic ring and work eight sc into the ring. End with a slip stitch. For the next round, you will chain one and increase in all of the stitches and finish the round with a slip stitch. In the third round, you will chain one, crochet sc in one stitch and an increase in the next. You will repeat this until the end of the round and end the round with a slip stitch.

For the fourth round, work sc in each of the following two stitches and increase in the next one. Repeat this until the end of the round. For the fifth round, you will chain three that we won't count as a stitch and then crochet dc in the next three stitches and increase by working two dc into the following stitch. You will repeat this until the end of the round. End the round with a slip stitch into the top of the chain from the beginning of the round. Do not fasten off the yarn just yet.

For the assembly, you will first attach the tentacles to the bottom part of the jellyfish body. You will do this by pulling the tails through the stitches of the bottom part and tie them together.

It is that easy. You can secure them if you feel it is necessary. Then you will place the eyes and embroider the mouth. You can position these wherever you want. Next, you will connect the top and the bottom part of the jellyfish.

You will take the excess yarn from the bottom part and pull the loop through one of the stitches on the top part. Next, you will work sc through both the top and bottom part stitches at once to connect them together. Once you have almost reached the end of the round, insert the stuffing into the body of the jellyfish and finish the round by sc.

To finish the jellyfish, you will work shell stitch all around the connection area. You will work 5-6 dc in one stitch, skip three stitches and repeat. You will do this until the end of the round. End the round with a slip stitch to the base and fasten off the yarn. Weave in the ends and you have finished your jellyfish amigurumi. Isn't it adorable?

Glossary

To read crochet patterns, you will have to memorize a lot of abbreviations or have detailed glossaries at hand. This is not a problem. On the web, you can find many of them in different languages. The best suggestion at this point is to stick to simple patterns. If you cannot understand the abbreviations, it is very likely that you did not master crocheting enough to create that project. It is a good idea to create your own glossary too, with the abbreviations you want and use most, including those that your brain does not want to memorize.

Crochet abbreviations:

SC- Single crochet

DC - Double crochet

TR - Treble crochet

YO– Yarn over

CL– Cluster

WS and RS tell you whether you should be working on the "wrong" side or the "right side".

CH– Chainlink

This is all basic. Most patterns have glossaries included, which show you what all the abbreviations mean, so do not be worried about them.

Conclusion

Crocheting is an age-old practice that was passed down for generations, primarily through mothers to their daughters, but it has become increasingly inclusive, with men also getting into the practice. For a beginner, it is advised that you avoid expensive yarns. Inexpensive yarns should be your friend. You should also avoid slippery yarns as well as anything with texture. As a beginner, textured yarns will make everything to be hard because it will be difficult for you to see your stitches. You are likely to be frustrated when you are not able to see your stitches. It is therefore recommended that you use smooth acrylic yarn that has a medium weight. Again, it is only by practicing that you will become perfect in this field. Crocheting is an enjoyable hobby, and I hope you will always have the desire to crochet during your free time.

Generally, you also have to learn about ethics and yarn. This means that you have taken a considerable amount of your time to understand how you can make sustainable yarn choices that will touch on things like vegan yarn and organic yarn. There are also other yarn decisions that will relate to your personal ethics and beliefs around the society, the environment, and animals around. For instance, my personal ethics will not allow me to crochet something like a thong because my perception of it concerning the society around me is negative or rather considered immoral. Therefore, before doing some projects, you have to put some considerations as well.

The best way for you to find it easy to learn how to crochet is by having to make a good hook choice. However, the challenge that most beginners do encounter comes when choosing the right hook. Every person has his/her preferences and therefore, what may seem suitable for one person may not be suitable for another person. Furthermore, different projects and different yarns will require hooks of different styles, sizes, and shapes. Don't be scared by this. After doing your first few projects, you will be able to identify the best hook that fits you.

Understanding the anatomy of the hook will help you made the right decisions when choosing hooks for different projects.

Taking small breaks in between your crocheting and exercising, we also have some more tips that can help you to be careful while crocheting. Our hand posture plays a big role in crocheting. Sometimes ignoring the crochet basics can be the cause of our hand and wrist pains. Our bodies are always communicating with us if only we could listen. If you strain any part of the body, you will experience some discomfort. When crocheting, to avoid the pains mentioned above, how should we position our hand? Some people are fond of flexing their wrists even when crocheting, but it is advisable always to keep them straight. You should make this a habit even if you are not crocheting. It might be hard at the beginning, but a wrist brace should come in hand and align the wrist.

Made in the USA
Coppell, TX
04 July 2022

79558894R00074